MEATMEN
COOKING CHANNEL

THE MEATMEN FAVOURITES

CHINESE · MALAY · INDIAN · EURASIAN · PERANAKAN

Marshall Cavendish
Cuisine

All photographs by The MeatMen Channel Pte Ltd
except for those on pages 2–3, 6–11 and the back cover

Editor: Lydia Leong
Designer: Bernard Go Kwang Meng
Food Preparation: Tan Junjie and Sharon Gonzago

Published by Marshall Cavendish Cuisine
An imprint of Marshall Cavendish International

A member of the
Times Publishing Group

Other Marshall Cavendish Offices:
Marshall Cavendish Corporation. 99 White Plains Road, Tarrytown NY 10591-9001,
USA • Marshall Cavendish International (Thailand) Co Ltd. 253 Asoke, 12th Flr,
Sukhumvit 21 Road, Klongtoey Nua, Wattana, Bangkok 10110, Thailand • Marshall
Cavendish (Malaysia) Sdn Bhd, Times Subang, Lot 46, Subang Hi-Tech Industrial
Park, Batu Tiga, 40000 Shah Alam, Selangor Darul Ehsan, Malaysia

Marshall Cavendish is a registered trademark of Times Publishing Limited

National Library Board, Singapore Cataloguing-in-Publication Data

Name(s): MeatMen Cooking Channel.
Title: The MeatMen favourites / MeatMen.
Other title(s): MeatMen Cooking Channel | Meat Men favourites
Description: Singapore : Marshall Cavendish Cuisine, [2017]
Identifier(s): OCN 971983651 | ISBN 978-981-47-5165-0 (paperback)
Subject(s): LCSH: Cooking, Singaporean. | Cooking, Asian. | Cookbooks.
Classification: DDC 641.595957--dc23

Printed by Times Offset (M) Sdn Bhd

DEDICATION

This book is for our fans who are ever-passionate about Singaporean cooking — this book would not have been possible without you!

It is also for our loved ones who have allowed us the time to pursue this passion of ours.

CONTENTS

ACKNOWLEDGEMENTS

Our source of inspiration continues to be all those who love and appreciate food. You have been our key encouragement and the reason why we continue to pursue better recipes each and every day. Thank you for making this compilation of MeatMen favourites possible.

The MeatMen Cooking Channel

INTRODUCTION

In Singapore, we have the best of Chinese, Malay, Indian, Eurasian and Peranakan cultures and their cuisines. We can boast of a seemingly endless array of dishes, each one detailing a rich heritage of Asian flavours.

In *MeatMen Favourites*, we feature some of our best-loved dishes, as well as the dishes most requested by fellow home cooks on our social media channels. These dishes are as authentic and real as you can get without needing fancy equipment or skills, and prepared in the comfort of your own home.

ABOUT THE MEATMEN COOKING CHANNEL

We are simply a bunch of greedy guys in the creative trade who love their food, be it eating, cooking, growing or even capturing it on film.

It all started with the obsession to record the whole process of food creation through the lens. That passion soon spread and before long, we were infected with the food-frenzy craze.

We are about being simple. Our vision is simple, to prove that cooking at home is not difficult. We hope to simplify it for everyone to make cooking easy and fun for all.

The MeatMen Cooking Channel symbolises a vision we have to bring awesome local dish dishes from hawker centres and coffee shops to the comfort of our own homes.

Chris Lim

Kiat Yingda

Tan Junjie

Jonathan Tan

FAVOURITE CHINESE DISHES

A very old dish, goes back hundreds of years. Tender succulent chicken infused with the flavours from the lotus leaf, herbs stuffed in its cavity baked inside dough crust.

BEGGAR'S CHICKEN

Serves 6–8

75 g (2²/₃ oz) salt

50 g (1³/₄ oz) sugar

1 litre (32 fl oz / 4 cups) water, or as needed

1 whole chicken, 1–1.2 kg (2 lb 3 oz–2 lb 6 oz)

STUFFING

15 g (¹/₂ oz) *dang gui* (angelica root)

20 g (²/₃ oz) *gou qi* (Chinese wolfberries)

30 g (1 oz) *dang shen* (codonopsis root)

5 g (¹/₆ oz) *huang qi* (astragalus)

10 g (¹/₃ oz) *yu zhu* (Solomon's seal)

5 g (¹/₆ oz) *chuan xiong* (lovage)

20 g (²/₃ oz) dried scallops

6 red dates, pitted

3 dried Chinese mushrooms, soaked to soften

2 Tbsp Chinese rice wine (*hua tiao jiu*)

4 Tbsp chicken stock

SEASONING

1 Tbsp powdered rock sugar

1 tsp salt

¹/₂ tsp ground white pepper

1 Tbsp light soy sauce

1 Tbsp thick dark soy sauce

1 Tbsp Chinese rice wine (*hua tiao jiu*)

2 Tbsp sesame oil

DOUGH

1.5 kg (3 lb 4¹/₂ oz) plain flour

3 Tbsp salt

900 ml (30 fl oz) water

3 dried lotus leaves, soaked overnight

1. In a large pot, dissolve salt and sugar in 1 litre (32 fl oz / 4 cups) water to make a brine. Place chicken in brine, ensuring it is fully submerged. Add up to 500 ml (16 fl oz / 2 cups) if needed. Leave chicken to brine in fridge for up to 4 hours. Remove chicken from brining solution and pat dry.

2. Place all ingredients for stuffing in a steamer and steam for 15 minutes.

3. Mix ingredients for seasoning in a bowl. Rub seasoning all over chicken and cavity of chicken.

4. Place steamed stuffing into cavity of chicken along with any steaming liquid. Set aside.

5. Mix flour, salt and water to form a pliable dough. Add more water as necessary. Cover and rest dough for 30 minutes.

6. Preheat oven to 180°C (350°F).

7. Roll rested dough into a thick rectangle, wide enough to wrap chicken. Wrap chicken with lotus leaves making sure it is well sealed. Wrap and seal lotus leaf-wrapped chicken with dough.

8. Place wrapped chicken on a roasting tray and bake for 3 hours. Let chicken rest for 30 minutes before unwrapping. Serve.

A good dish of braised duck requires patience and a handful of essential aromatics!
In addition to the typical cinnamon sticks, star anise and cloves, we included *chuan xiong* and
dried mandarin peel for a more robust flavour. We know you'll love this dish because we do!

BRAISED DUCK

Serves 6–8

1 large duck

100 g (3¹⁄₂ oz) coarse salt

Water, as needed

4 Tbsp cooking oil

6 Tbsp brown sugar

60 g (2 oz) rock sugar

10 cloves garlic, peeled

10 shallots, peeled

50 g (1³⁄₄ oz) ginger, peeled
  and thickly sliced

50 g (1³⁄₄ oz) galangal, peeled
  and thickly sliced

5 cinnamon sticks

5 star anise

5 slices *chuan xiong* (lovage)

20 cloves

5 slices dried mandarin peel

2 Tbsp black peppercorns

250 ml (8 fl oz / 1 cup) sweet
  dark soy sauce

125 ml (4 fl oz / ¹⁄₂ cup) light
  soy sauce

SEASONING (adjusted to taste)

375 ml (12 fl oz 1¹⁄₂ cups)
  sweet dark soy sauce

250 ml (8 fl oz / 1 cup) light
  soy sauce

3 Tbsp salt, or to taste

Sugar, to taste

3 Tbsp oyster sauce

2 Tbsp Chinese rice wine
  (*hua tiao jiu*)

1 Tbsp sesame oil

100 g (3¹⁄₂ oz) tapioca flour,
  mixed with some water

1. Rinse duck and remove excess fat at rear end. Rub well with coarse salt and set aside for 20 minutes. Rinse salt off duck, taking care to rinse any wax from under wings and thighs.

2. Boil 2 litres (64 fl oz / 8 cups) water and scald duck for 2 minutes. Drain and set aside in a braising pan.

3. Heat oil in a large wok over medium heat. Add brown sugar and rock sugar and cook until sugar is caramelised.

4. Add garlic, shallots, ginger, galangal, cinnamon sticks, star anise, *chuan xiong,* cloves, dried mandarin peel and peppercorns and stir-fry until fragrant.

5. Add sweet dark soy sauce and light soy sauce and bring to a boil.

6. Pour contents of wok over duck in braising pan. Add about 4 litres (128 fl oz / 16 cups) hot water or enough to submerge duck completely.

7. Add sweet dark soy sauce and light soy sauce, adjusting quantities according to taste and amount of water added to pan. Add salt and sugar to taste. Bring to a boil, then cover and braise over low heat for 1–1¹⁄₂ hours.

8. Remove duck from pan and let rest for 30 minutes.

9. Strain braising liquid and discard spices. Skim off layer of oil. Measure out 2 litres (64 fl oz / 8 cups) braising liquid and add to a clean pan.

10. Add oyster sauce, Chinese rice wine and sesame oil and bring to a boil. Lower heat and thicken braising liquid with tapioca flour mixed with water. Adjust the amount of water used according to how thick you want the sauce to be.

11. Cut duck into serving portions and arrange on a large serving plate. Ladle gravy over and garnish as desired. Serve with sliced cucumbers if desired.

Pork ribs braised in *bak kut teh* stock and stir-fried with a rich, dark caramel sauce. The dried chillies give it an additional kick and the shredded dried squid add an unbeatable umami flavour. Enjoy with a bowl of piping hot steamed white rice.

DRY BAK KUT TEH

Serves 6–8

1 kg (2 lb 3 oz) pork ribs

Water, as needed

4 dried Chinese mushrooms, soaked to soften

1 bulb garlic

1 packet *bak kut teh* spices

Cooking oil, as needed

20 g (²/₃ oz) dried shredded cuttlefish, rinsed

6 dried chillies, soaked to soften and cut into 5-cm (2-in) lengths

1 medium onion, peeled and cut into quarters

6 cloves garlic, peeled

3 ladies' fingers, cut diagonally into 0.5-cm (¹/₄-in) thick slices

Salt, to taste

Ground white pepper, to taste

HERBS

20 g (²/₃ oz) *dang shen* (codonopsis root)

10 g (¹/₃ oz) *shu di huang* (rehmannia root)

10 g (¹/₃ oz) *gou qi* (Chinese wolfberries)

3 g (¹/₁₀ oz) *dang gui* (angelica root)

3 g (¹/₁₀ oz) *chuan xiong* (lovage)

20 g (²/₃ oz) *yu zhu* (Solomon's seal)

SAUCE

1 Tbsp sweet dark soy sauce

2 tsp light soy sauce

1 tsp sugar

1 tsp salt

1. Blanch pork ribs in a pot of boiling water for 5 minutes, then rinse under running water.

2. Rinse herbs.

3. Boil 1.5 litres (48 fl oz / 6 cups) water in a pot and add pork ribs, dried Chinese mushrooms, garlic, *bak kut teh* spices and herbs. Simmer over low heat for 45 minutes.

4. Add ingredients for sauce and continue to simmer until liquid is almost dried out. Remove cooked pork ribs and discard rest of ingredients. Set aside until needed.

5. Heat some oil in a wok over medium heat and deep-fry dried shredded cuttlefish until crisp. Drain well and set aside.

6. Reheat 2 Tbsp oil in the wok and add dried chillies, onion and garlic. Stir-fry until fragrant.

7. Add cooked pork ribs, ladies' fingers and half the fried shredded cuttlefish. Stir-fry until ladies' fingers are done. Season with salt and pepper to taste.

8. Dish out and garnish with remaining fried shredded cuttlefish. Serve.

For all meat lovers out there. Imagine biting into crispy, crunchy crackling and sweet, juicy succulent meat. Resistance is futile. You've simply got to try this.

SIO BAK ROAST PORK BELLY

Serves 6–8

2 kg (4 lb 6 oz) pork belly

2 cubes fermented
  red bean curd

1 Tbsp five-spice powder

1 Tbsp sea salt

1 Tbsp ground white pepper

1 Tbsp coarse sea salt

2 Tbsp white vinegar

1 Tbsp Chinese rice wine
  (*hua tiao jiu*)

1 tsp sugar

1. Start preparations a day ahead.

2. Wash pork belly and pat dry. Prick pork belly skin well using a meat pricker. This will ensure that the skin is crisp after roasting.

3. In a bowl, mix fermented red bean curd, five-spice powder, sea salt and pepper into a paste. Apply paste on underside of pork belly.

4. Rub coarse sea salt and vinegar evenly onto skin.

5. Skewer pork belly with metal skewers to keep meat flat while it roasts.

6. Place pork belly on a wire rack in a roasting tray and leave to marinate, uncovered, in the refrigerator overnight. This is to draw out moisture from the skin.

7. Preheat oven to its highest setting.

8. Place pork belly in the middle rack of the oven. Roast for 30 minutes.

9. Lower oven temperature to 200°C (400°F) and continue roasting for 1 hour 15 minutes.

10. Remove pork belly from oven and scrape off any charred bits.

11. Remove metal skewers and let pork belly rest for 30 minutes before slicing to serve.

This traditional Ampang Hakka *yong tau foo* recipe is the real deal, with minced pork, dried prawns and salted fish added to the stuffing. The stuffed vegetables and bean curd are then fried to a lovely golden brown and served in a rich fermented black bean gravy.

AMPANG YONG TAU FOO

Serves 4–6

400 g (14¹/₃ oz) or 2 pieces firm bean curd (*tau kwa*)

3 large tofu puffs (*tau pok*)

¹/₂ medium bitter gourd

1 medium aubergine (eggplant/brinjal)

2 red chillies

2 green chillies

Cooking oil, as needed

FILLING

20 g (²/₃ oz) dried prawns, rinsed

30 g (1 oz) salted fish

400 g (14¹/₃ oz) store-bought unsalted mackerel fish paste

300 g (11 oz) minced pork with at least 30% fat

¹/₄ tsp sugar

¹/₄ tsp ground white pepper

SAUCE

2 Tbsp cooking oil

6 cloves garlic, peeled and minced

1¹/₂ Tbsp fermented black beans

375 ml (12 fl oz / 1¹/₂ cups) water

1¹/₂ Tbsp oyster sauce

1 Tbsp Chinese rice wine (*hua tiao jiu*)

1 tsp sugar

2 tsp dried sole powder

¹/₄ tsp ground white pepper

2 Tbsp cornflour, mixed with 2 Tbsp water

1. Cut firm bean curd and tofu puffs into 2 triangles each. Cut bitter gourd into 1.5-cm (³/₄-in) thick rings. Cut aubergine into 3-cm (1¹/₄-in) thick slices, then make a slit in the middle without cutting through. Make a slit in each chilli and remove seeds. Set *yong tau foo* items aside.

2. Prepare filling. Dry-fry dried prawns in a wok over medium heat until fragrant. Set aside to cool. Repeat to dry-fry salted fish.

3. Mince toasted dried prawns and place in a bowl with toasted salted. Add remaining ingredients for filling, then use chopsticks to stir mixture well in a single direction until filling is very sticky and it becomes hard to stir.

4. Scoop filling up with one hand and throw it against the bowl several times until it takes on a springy texture.

5. Stuff prepared *yong tau foo* items with filling.

6. Heat sufficient oil for deep-frying and deep-fry stuffed *yong tau foo* items until cooked and golden brown. Alternatively, use an air-fryer set at 200°C (400°F). Arrange fried items on a large serving plate.

7. Prepare sauce. Heat oil in a wok over medium heat. Add garlic and stir-fry until fragrant. Add fermented black beans and stir-fry again until fragrant. Add water, oyster sauce, Chinese rice wine, sugar, dried sole powder and pepper. Stir to mix. Lower heat and simmer for 5 minutes. Adjust seasoning to taste. Stir in cornflour solution to thicken sauce.

8. Ladle sauce over fried *yong tau foo* items and serve.

This is a traditional Hakka dish that is seldom found at food stalls and restaurants, and is usually prepared at home. The springy yam-rich abacus beads absorb the flavours of the other ingredients and you get all the different tastes and textures in one mouthful!

ABACUS BEADS WITH MINCED PORK

Serves 6–8

3 Tbsp cooking oil

100 g (3½ oz) minced pork

20 g (⅔ oz) dried prawns, rinsed and finely chopped

40 g (1⅓ oz) shallots, peeled and minced

4 cloves garlic, peeled and minced

3 Tbsp *chye poh* (salted radish), rinsed

4 dried Chinese mushrooms, soaked to soften, thinly sliced

10 g (⅓ oz) shredded dried cuttlefish

10 g (⅓ oz) dried wood ear fungus, soaked to soften and thinly sliced

20 g (⅔ oz) Beijing cabbage

1–2 bird's eye chillies (*cili padi*), sliced

1 spring onion, sliced

1 Tbsp crisp-fried shallots

ABACUS BEADS

400 g (14⅓ oz) yam, peeled and cut into cubes

120 g (4⅓ oz) tapioca flour

¼ tsp salt

85 ml (2½ fl oz / ⅓ cup) boiling water

2 Tbsp cooking oil

SEASONING

2 Tbsp light soy sauce

1 Tbsp oyster sauce

2 Tbsp Chinese rice wine (*hua tiao jiu*)

Salt, to taste

Ground white pepper, to taste

1. Prepare abacus beads. Place yam in a steamer and steam until soft. While still hot, mash yam and mix with tapioca flour and salt. Add boiling water and knead to form a pliable dough.

2. Roll dough into a long strip and cut into 5 g (⅙ oz) pieces. Using your hands, roll each piece of dough into a ball, then use a finger to make a depression in the centre

3. Boil a pot of water and add abacus beads, When they float, scoop them out with a slotted spoon and place in a bowl. Drizzle with oil to prevent the beads from sticking. Set aside.

4. Heat oil in a wok over medium heat. Add minced pork, dried prawns, shallots and garlic. Stir-fry until fragrant.

5. Add *chye poh* and dried Chinese mushrooms and continue to stir-fry until fragrant.

6. Add shredded dried cuttlefish, dried wood ear fungus and cabbage. Stir-fry until cabbage is softened.

7. Add abacus seeds and seasoning. Mix well.

8. Dish out and garnish with chopped bird's eye chillies, spring onion and crisp-fried shallots. Serve.

FAVOURITE MALAY DISHES

Chicken Rendang	30
Ikan Pari Masak Assam Pedas	32
Lontong Sayur Lodeh	34
Nasi Kerabu	36
Pulut Inti Udang	38
Kueh Dadar	40

Rendang is a traditional Malay dish that goes well with rice.
It is gently simmered for a long time until the meat is meltingly tender
and the rich flavour of the spices and coconut milk infuses the meat.

CHICKEN RENDANG

Serves 6–8

1 whole chicken, 1–1.2 kg
(2 lb 3 oz–2 lb 6 oz)

200 g (7 oz) grated coconut

4 Tbsp cooking oil

1 Tbsp chopped palm sugar

400 ml (14 fl oz / 1³/₄ cups)
coconut milk

2 turmeric leaves, finely
sliced

4 kaffir lime leaves,
finely sliced

2 stalks lemongrass, ends
trimmed and bruised

3 dried *assam* slices
(*assam gelugur*)

1 tsp salt

SPICE PASTE

12 dried chillies, soaked
to soften

150 g (5¹/₃ oz) shallots,
peeled

2 cloves garlic, peeled

20 g (²/₃ oz) ginger, peeled

50 g (1³/₄ oz) lemongrass,
ends trimmed

30 g (1 oz) galangal, peeled

3 candlenuts

1. Rinse chicken and cut into 8 pieces.

2. In a wok, dry-fry grated coconut until golden
   brown. Set aside to cool. Using a food processor,
   blend toasted grated coconut, stopping
   occasionally to scrape the sides down. Repeat
   until oil begins to separate from the solids and
   mixture takes on the look of peanut butter.
   Remove to a bowl and set aside.

3. Using the food processor, blend ingredients for
   spice paste until fine. Remove to another bowl.

4. Heat oil in a wok over medium heat. Add
   spice paste and palm sugar. Stir-fry for about
   15 minutes or until oil starts to separate.

5. Add chicken and stir-fry for 5 minutes. Add
   grated coconut and mix well.

6. Add coconut milk, turmeric leaves, kaffir lime
   leaves, lemongrass and dried *assam* slices.
   Season with salt. Lower heat and simmer gently
   for 45 minutes or until chicken is cooked through
   and gravy is reduced.

7. Taste and adjust seasoning as necessary.
   Dish out and serve.

TIP   As a variation to this recipe, chicken can be substituted with
       beef or mutton. Frying the spice paste can fill your kitchen
       with a pungent cooking smell. To avoid this, just mix the
       ingredients instead of frying, and cook on a slow simmer
       until the gravy is dry and the meat is tender.

This spicy and sour tamarind-based fish curry is fragrant with the flavours of the laksa leaves and torch ginger bud. Bilimbi is a local seasonal fruit that imparts a piquant sour flavour to the dish.

IKAN PARI MASAK ASSAM PEDAS

Serves 4–6

1 stalk lemongrass, ends trimmed and bruised

50 g (1³/₄ oz) tamarind paste

200 ml (6³/₄ fl oz) water

20 laksa leaves

1 anchovy stock cube

2 tsp sugar, or to taste

Salt, to taste

500 g (1 lb 1¹/₂ oz) stingray, cut into small pieces

10 ladies' fingers

1 large red onion, peeled, cut into quarters and layers separated

1 torch ginger bud, halved

3 dried *assam* slices (*assam gelugur*)

10 bilimbi, cut into halves

1 tomato, cut into wedges

SPICE PASTE

4 Tbsp cooking oil

15 dried chillies, soaked to soften

4 red chillies

120 g (4¹/₃ oz) shallots, peeled

4 cloves garlic, peeled

1 stalk lemongrass, ends trimmed and bruised

1 Tbsp *belacan* (dried prawn paste), toasted

5 g (¹/₆ oz) turmeric, peeled

5 g (¹/₆ oz) galangal

1. Prepare spice paste. Using a food processor, blend all ingredients for spice paste except oil until fine.

2. Heat oil in a wok over medium heat. Add spice paste and lemongrass, and stir-fry until oil starts to separate from the solids and paste is fragrant.

3. Mix tamarind paste with 200 ml (6³/₄ fl oz) water and strain. Add to wok and bring to a simmer.

4. Add laksa leaves and anchovy stock cube. Mix well. Taste and season with sugar and salt.

5. Add stingray to gravy. When stingray is almost done, add ladies' fingers, onion, torch ginger bud, dried *assam* slices, bilimbi and tomato. Continue to simmer until stingray is cooked through.

6. Dish out, garnish as desired and serve.

A delicious all-in-one meal that includes rice, vegetables and protein-rich ingredients. *Lontong* is a compressed rice cake made from boiling rice wrapped in banana leaves. When cooked, the rice takes on the flavour of the banana leaves. Here, it is served with a rich vegetable stew.

LONTONG SAYUR LODEH

Serves 6–8

400 g (14¹⁄₃ oz) or 2 pieces firm bean curd (*tau kwa*)

80 g (2⁴⁄₅ oz) tempeh

Cooking oil, as needed

1 litre (32 fl oz / 4 cups) coconut milk

200 g (7 oz) white cabbage, cut into large chunks

5 long beans, cut into 5-cm (2-in) lengths

200 g (7 oz) yam bean, peeled and cut into 5-cm (2-in) sticks

1 carrot, peeled and cut into 5-cm (2-in) sticks

20 g (²⁄₃ oz) glass noodles

50 g (1³⁄₄ oz) dried bean curd sticks

250 ml (8 fl oz / 1 cup) coconut cream

1¹⁄₂ tsp salt, or to taste

¹⁄₂ tsp sugar, or to taste

500 g (1 lb 1¹⁄₂ oz) store-bought *lontong* (compressed rice cake)

SPICE PASTE

4 dried chillies, soaked to soften

120 g (4¹⁄₃ oz) shallots, peeled

4 cloves garlic, peeled

2 candlenuts

2 stalks lemongrass, ends trimmed

30 g (1 oz) turmeric, peeled

10 g (¹⁄₃ oz) galangal, peeled

40 g (1¹⁄₃ oz) dried prawns

1 tsp *belacan* (dried prawn paste), toasted

1. Cut firm bean curd into 4 triangles each. Cut tempeh into 3-cm (1¹⁄₄-in) strips. Heat some oil in a wok over medium heat and fry firm bean curd until golden brown. Drain and set aside. Repeat to fry tempeh until crispy. Drain and set aside.

2. Using a food processor, blend all ingredients for spice paste until fine.

3. Leave 4 Tbsp oil in wok and reheat over medium heat. Add spice paste and stir-fry for 4–5 minutes until fragrant.

4. Lower heat and add coconut milk. Bring to a simmer. Do not allow coconut milk to boil as it will curdle.

5. Add cabbage, long beans, yam bean and carrot. Simmer until vegetables are until tender.

6. Add glass noodles, dried bean curd sticks and fried firm bean curd. Stir in coconut cream. Season with salt and sugar.

7. Cut *lontong* into slices and place in a large serving bowl. Ladle vegetable curry over. Top with fried tempeh, garnish as desired and serve.

This Malay dish originates from Kelantan, a northern state in Malaysia.
The rice is cooked to a rich blue hue using colouring obtained from the dried blue pea flower,
and served with various side dishes which are tossed together like a salad.

NASI KERABU

Serves 4–6

KERABU RICE

400 g (14¹/₃ oz) rice

30 dried blue pea flowers

500 ml (16 fl oz / 2 cups) hot water

1 stalk lemongrass, ends trimmed and bruised

2 kaffir lime leaves

2 slices ginger

2 slices galangal

FISH SAMBAL

Cooking oil for deep-frying

2 hard tail scad (*ikan cencaru*)

4 Tbsp grated coconut, toasted and pounded

4 Tbsp fried dried shrimp (*udang geragau*), pounded

Salt, to taste

Ground white pepper, to taste

SPICE PASTE

3 Tbsp cooking oil

60 g (2 oz) shallots, peeled

1 clove garlic, peeled

1 tsp *belacan* (dried prawn paste), toasted

1 stalk lemongrass, ends trimmed and bruised

¹/₂ tsp sugar

¹/₄ tsp salt

ACCOMPANIMENTS

200 g (7 oz) bean sprouts

A handful of thinly sliced laksa leaves, torch ginger bud and lemongrass

200 g (7 oz) winged beans

2 salted eggs, hard-boiled

Fish crackers, as desired

Sambal belacan, as desired

1. Prepare *kerabu* rice. Rinse rice and place in a rice cooker. Soak blue pea flowers in hot water for 30 minutes to extract colour. Strain and discard flowers. Add blue pea flower water, lemongrass, kaffir lime leaves, ginger and galangal to rice cooker. Let sit for 15 minutes before turning rice cooker on to cook rice.

2. Prepare fish sambal. Heat oil for deep-frying and deep-fry fish until cooked and golden brown. Skin and debone fish. Flake flesh and set aside.

3. Prepare spice paste. Using a food processor, blend all ingredients for spice paste except oil until fine. Heat oil in a wok over medium heat and fry spice paste until oil starts to separate and paste is fragrant.

4. Add flaked fish, pounded grated coconut and pounded fried dried shrimp. Season with salt and pepper. Mix until well combined.

5. Arrange *kerabu* rice, fish sambal and accompaniments on a large serving plate for guests to help themselves to. Toss rice with fish sambal and accompaniments before eating.

Steamed glutinous rice fragrant with coconut milk, enclosing a spicy grated coconut and dried prawn filling, wrapped with banana leaves and grilled to impart an appetising smoked flavour. This favourite Malay treat is perfect as a snack any time of the day.

PULUT INTI UDANG

Makes 22 pieces

22 banana leaf sheets, each about 18 x 18-cm (7 x 7-in)

COCONUT FILLING

4 Tbsp cooking oil

1 tsp sugar

Salt, to taste

Lime juice, to taste

100 g (3$\frac{1}{2}$ oz) dried prawns, finely chopped

200 g (7 oz) grated skinned coconut

SPICE PASTE FOR COCONUT FILLING

80 g (2$\frac{4}{5}$ oz) shallots, peeled

2 cloves garlic, peeled

8 dried chillies, soaked to soften

1 Tbsp fennel powder

1 stalk lemongrass, ends trimmed

20 g ($\frac{2}{3}$ oz) turmeric, peeled

GLUTINOUS RICE

30 dried blue pea flowers

4 Tbsp hot water

600 g (1 lb 5$\frac{1}{3}$ oz) glutinous rice, soaked for 4 hours and drained before use

4 slices ginger

4 pandan leaves, knotted

200 ml (6$\frac{3}{4}$ fl oz) water

300 ml (10 fl oz / 1$\frac{1}{4}$ cups) coconut milk

1 tsp salt

1. Prepare spice paste for coconut filling. Using a food processor, blend all ingredients for spice paste until smooth.

2. Prepare coconut filling. Heat oil a wok over medium heat. Add spice paste and sugar and stir-fry until oil starts to separate and the paste is fragrant. Season with salt and lime juice.

3. Add dried prawns and stir-fry for 1 minute. Lower heat and add grated coconut. Stir-fry until mixture is slightly dry. Dish out and set aside.

4. Prepare glutinous rice. Soak dried blue pea flowers in 4 Tbsp hot water for about 20 minutes. Strain and discard flowers. Set blue pea flower water aside.

5. Place soaked glutinous rice in a steamer with ginger and pandan leaves. Steam for 20 minutes.

6. Mix 200 ml (6$\frac{3}{4}$ fl oz) water into rice and steam for another 10 minutes.

7. Repeat to mix coconut milk into rice and steam for 5 minutes.

8. Drizzle blue pea flower water over glutinous rice. Mix to get a marbling effect. Continue to steam until glutinous rice is cooked. Set aside to cool.

9. Make banana leaves pliable by running each sheet over an open fire.

10. Spoon 3 Tbsp glutinous rice down the centre of a banana leaf. Flatten rice slightly, then spoon 3 tsp coconut filling in a line over rice. Roll banana leaf up to enclose rice and filling. Secure open ends of leaf with toothpicks. Repeat to make more parcels until ingredients are used up.

11. Grill parcels in a non-stick pan over medium heat until banana leaves char a little or use your oven's grill mode and grill at 230°C (450°F) for 4 minutes on each side.

12. Serve.

Moist grated coconut caramelised with fragrant palm sugar
and wrapped in a thin pandan-flavoured crepe. Need we say more?

KUEH DADAR

Makes about 12 pieces

COCONUT FILLING

1 kg (2 lb 3 oz) skinned grated coconut

200 g (7 oz) palm sugar, grated

2 Tbsp sugar

$\frac{1}{2}$ tsp salt

2 pandan leaves, knotted

3 Tbsp water

PANDAN CREPE BATTER

20 pandan leaves

200 ml ($6\frac{3}{4}$ fl oz) water

200 g (7 oz) plain flour

A pinch of salt

2 eggs

560 ml ($18\frac{2}{3}$ fl oz) coconut milk

1 Tbsp cooking oil

1. Prepare coconut filling. Add all ingredients for coconut filling to a wok and cook over low heat until sugar is melted and mixture comes together. The filling should be moist. Set aside to cool.

2. Prepare pandan juice for pandan crepe batter. Using a food processor, blend pandan leaves with 200 ml ($6\frac{3}{4}$ fl oz) water. Strain juice through a muslin cloth. Discard fibre.

3. Place all ingredients for pandan crepe batter into the food processor and blend until smooth. Strain to remove any lumps. The consistency of the batter should be like that of single cream. Let batter rest for 30 minutes before cooking.

4. Heat a non-stick pan over medium heat. Wipe pan with some kitchen paper dipped in oil.

5. Ladle some batter into pan, then tilt pan around to create a thin and even crepe. Quickly pour any excess batter into a bowl and return pan to the heat. Leave crepe to cook undisturbed for about 30 seconds, then transfer crepe to a plate. Make about 12 crepes.

6. Spoon about 4 Tbsp coconut filling on the centre of a crepe. Fold 2 opposite sides of crepe over filling, then roll up like a spring roll. Repeat for remaining ingredients.

7. Serve.

FAVOURITE INDIAN DISHES

Although this is usually cooked in a tandoor, it can also be easily cooked in a home oven. Marinating the meat overnight, tenderises it while infusing it with the rich flavour of the spices. Make sure you achieve the charred bits at the edges, as this gives the smoked flavour that screams tandoori!

TANDOORI CHICKEN

Serves 4–6

1 whole chicken, 1–1.2 kg
(2 lb 3 oz–2 lb 6 oz), skinned
and cut into 8 pieces

MARINADE

350 ml (11²/₃ fl oz) yoghurt

1 Tbsp lemon juice

4 Tbsp ghee

60 g (2 oz) shallot paste
(made by blending shallots)

1 Tbsp ginger paste
(made by blending ginger)

1 Tbsp garlic paste
(made by blending garlic)

2 tsp garam masala

2 tsp chilli powder

1 tsp sugar

2 tsp salt

GARNISH

Lemon wedges

Sliced cucumbers

Mint leaves

1. Start preparations a day ahead. Mix ingredients for marinade in a bowl. Reserve 2 Tbsp for basting and rub remaining marinade over chicken. Cover and leave chicken to marinate overnight in the fridge.

2. Preheat oven to 180°C (350°F).

3. Thread chicken pieces through metal skewers and roast in the oven for 30 minutes using the rotisserie function.

4. Remove and baste chicken using reserved marinade.

5. Return chicken to the oven and continue roasting for another 30 minutes or until chicken is cooked through and there are charred bits at the edges.

6. Remove skewers and arrange chicken on a serving plate. Serve with lemon wedges and sliced cucumbers. Garnish with mint leaves.

Juicy and tender chunks of mutton cooked Indian-style. Like all curries, mutton masala will taste better with keeping as this allows the flavours to mature. Store refrigerated overnight and reheat over low heat to avoid burning. Enjoy with naan or basmati rice.

MUTTON MASALA

Serves 4–6

Ghee, as needed

1 Tbsp ginger paste
(made by blending ginger)

1 Tbsp garlic paste
(made by blending garlic)

½ tsp turmeric powder

1 kg (2 lb 3 oz) mutton,
cut into pieces

Water, as needed

3 Tbsp yoghurt

1 tsp salt

1 tsp sugar

6 stalks curry leaves, leaves
plucked, stalks discarded

SPICE PASTE

10 dried Kashmiri chillies
or regular dried chillies,
soaked to soften

6 dried chillies, soaked
to soften

1 Tbsp coriander seeds

1 Tbsp black peppercorns

1 tsp fennel

2 tsp cumin

5-cm (2-in) cinnamon stick

5 cloves

2 star anise

2 cloves garlic, peeled

20 g (⅔ oz) ginger, peeled

1½ Tbsp lemon juice

1. Using a food processor, blend all ingredients for spice paste until smooth. (Blend cinnamon, cloves and star anise separately in a spice mill if your food processor is unable to blend these hard spice sufficiently fine.) Transfer to a bowl and set aside.

2. Heat 3 Tbsp ghee in a pressure cooker. Add ginger paste, garlic paste and turmeric powder and stir-fry until fragrant.

3. Add mutton and stir-fry until meat changes colour.

4. Add in enough water to cover about three-quarters of the mutton. Cover pressure cooker and cook for 30 minutes.

5. Strain and reserve mutton stock. Set cooked mutton aside.

6. Heat 4 Tbsp ghee in a pot over medium heat. Add spice paste and stir-fry until oil separates from paste. Add yoghurt and mix well.

7. Add reserved mutton stock, salt, sugar and cooked mutton and stir-fry for 6 minutes.

8. Add curry leaves and continue to stir-fry until liquid is reduced and thick.

9. Dish out, garnish as desired and serve.

TIP   If not using a pressure cooker, simmer the mutton until tender over the stove. We used Indian yoghurt for its thick consistency. A good substitute would be Greek yoghurt or any unflavoured yoghurt.

A luxurious one-dish meal that features fluffy saffron-infused basmati rice
with a light note of rose water. The fish masala is like a hidden treasure buried in the rice.

FISH BIRYANI

Serves 4–6

4 Spanish mackerel steaks, each about 125 g (4½ oz) and 1.5-cm (¾-in) thick
1 Tbsp turmeric powder
Salt, as needed
Cooking oil, as needed
3 Tbsp ghee
1 onion, peeled and sliced
6 cloves
4 cardamom pods
2 cinnamon sticks
½ tsp sugar
2 medium tomatoes, sliced
20 g (⅔ oz) cashew nuts

20 g (⅔ oz) almonds
3 Tbsp Indian yoghurt

SPICE PASTE
8 green chillies
5 garlic cloves, peeled
30 g (1 oz) ginger, peeled
1 onion, peeled and sliced
1 tsp cumin powder
1 tsp turmeric powder
1 tsp chilli powder
1 tsp garam masala
25 g (⅘ oz) coriander leaves (cilantro), chopped

RICE
4 litres (128 fl oz / 16 cups) water
1 tsp salt
3 pods cardamom
5 cloves
1 cinnamon stick
2 tsp ghee
500 g (1 lb 1½ oz) basmati rice, rinsed and soaked for 30 minutes
1 tsp rose water
5 Tbsp milk
A pinch of saffron

1. Rinse fish and pat dry. Rub well with turmeric powder and 1 tsp salt. Set aside to marinate for 15 minutes.

2. Heat 2 Tbsp oil in a pan and pan-fry fish until golden brown on one side before turning fish over to cook the other side. Remove and set aside.

3. Prepare spice paste. Using a food processor, blend all ingredients for spice paste until fine.

4. Heat ghee in a pot over medium heat. Add onion and stir-fry until golden brown. Add spice paste, cloves, cardamoms and cinnamon and stir-fry until oil separates from paste. Season with 1 tsp salt and sugar. Mix well.

5. Add tomatoes and simmer for about 10 minutes or until tomatoes are broken up.

6. In the meantime, blend cashews and almonds into a paste. Add to pot with yoghurt and simmer for 1 minute.

7. Gently place fried fish into pot and cover with gravy. Simmer gently for 5 minutes. Remove pot from heat and set aside.

8. Prepare rice. Boil 4 litres (128 fl oz / 16 cups) water in a large pot. Add salt, cardamoms, cloves and cinnamon. Lower heat and simmer for 5 minutes, then bring heat up to a boil. Add ghee, rice and rose water. Keep water at a rolling boil until rice is three-quarters done. Remove from heat and drain. Divide into 3 parts.

9. In another pot, heat milk with pinch of saffron. Set aside and let saffron steep in milk.

10. Using a large pot with a tight-fitting lid, spoon a third of rice into pot. Top with 2 fish steaks and spoon some gravy over. Layer with a second portion of rice to cover fish. Repeat to top with fish and gravy, followed by final portion of rice. Sprinkle with chopped coriander leaves and drizzle with saffron-infused milk.

11. Cover pot and place in an oven preheated to 200°C (400°F). Bake for 20–25 minutes.

12. Garnish with coriander and mint leaves if desired and serve.

Kurma is a rich Indian vegetable stew cooked in coconut milk and aromatic spices. Sometimes meat is added. A great side dish to biryani and Indian breads.

VEGETABLE KORMA

Serves 6–8

3 Tbsp cooking oil

2 cinnamon sticks

4 cardamom pods

4 cloves

1 tsp salt

4 Tbsp korma curry powder

1 tsp turmeric powder

500 ml (16 fl oz / 2 cups)
  water

50 g (1³/₄ oz) dhal, soaked
  for 30 minutes

3 potatoes, peeled and cut
  into quarters

1 small carrot, peeled
  and chopped

2 drumsticks, peeled and cut
  into 5-cm (2-in) lengths

100 g (3¹/₂ oz) cauliflower,
  cut into chunky florets

5 long beans, cut into 5-cm
  (2-in) lengths

1 medium aubergine
  (eggplant/brinjal), cut into
  5-cm (2-in) long pieces

4 green chillies, halved

2 tomatoes, cut into wedges

250 ml (8 fl oz / 1 cup)
  coconut milk

4 Tbsp yoghurt

SPICE PASTE

1 bulb garlic, peeled

50 g (1³/₄ oz) ginger, peeled

10 shallots, peeled

5 green chillies

1. Prepare spice paste. Using a food processor, blend all ingredients for spice paste until fine. Transfer to a bowl and set aside.

2. Heat oil in a pot over medium heat. Add cinnamon, cardamom and cloves and fry until cinnamon stick unfurls.

3. Add spice paste and stir-fry until fragrant.

4. Add salt, korma curry powder and turmeric powder and stir-fry for another minute.

5. Add 500 ml (16 fl oz / 2 cups) water and bring mixture to a boil.

6. Add soaked dhal, potatoes and carrot. Simmer until potatoes and carrot are almost tender.

7. Add drumsticks, cauliflower, long beans, aubergine, green chillies and half the tomatoes. Mix well.

8. Add coconut milk and simmer until vegetables are tender.

9. Add yoghurt and remaining tomatoes and simmer for a further 5 minutes. Adjust seasoning to taste.

10. Dish out and serve.

It takes some planning to prepare the rice and urad dhal batter as it requires several hours of soaking and resting time, but these thin and crispy South Indian crepes are well worth it! We suggest you enjoy these crepes with a simple coconut chutney. A perfect match indeed!

THOSAI

Makes about 12 pieces

THOSAI

400 g (13¹/₃ oz) rice, rinsed

200 g (7 oz) urad dhal (black lentils), rinsed

1 tsp fenugreek seeds, rinsed

180 g (6¹/₂ oz) day-old cooked rice, steamed for 10 minutes before using

1 tsp salt

1 tsp baking powder

Water, as needed

5 Tbsp melted ghee

COCONUT CHUTNEY

200 g (7 oz) grated skinned coconut

2 green chillies

1 medium onion, peeled and sliced

2 Tbsp cooking oil

1 tsp mustard seeds

4 dried chillies, soaked to soften

2 stalks curry leaves, leaves plucked, stalks discarded

1 tsp salt

1 tsp sugar

125 ml (4 fl oz / ¹/₂ cup) water

1. Start preparations for *thosai* 2 days ahead. Soak uncooked rice, urad dhal and fenugreek seeds in water overnight or for up to 12 hours.

2. Rinsed soaked ingredients and drain. Place in a food processor with cooked rice, salt and baking powder and blend into a smooth paste. Transfer to a bowl, cover and let rest in the refrigerator for up to 12 hours.

3. Prepare coconut chutney. Using a food processor, lightly blend grated coconut, green chillies and onion. Transfer to a bowl.

4. Heat oil in a pan over medium heat. Add mustard seeds and when seeds begin to pop, add dried chillies and curry leaves. Fry for a minute, then add blended coconut mixture. Season with salt and sugar. Add 125 ml (4 fl oz / ¹/₂ cup) water and simmer over low heat for 5 minutes. Set aside to serve with *thosai*.

5. To make *thosai,* heat a *thosai* pan or non-stick pan over medium heat. Brush pan with melted ghee.

6. Lightly stir *thosai* batter before using. Spoon a ladle of *thosai* batter into the centre of pan, then use the ladle to spread the batter into a circle in an outward circular motion. Turn up heat to medium-high. Sprinkle some ghee over *thosai* and around the edges as it cooks.

7. Cook until underside of *thosai* is crisp and golden brown. Fold in half while hot and transfer to a serving plate. Repeat to make more *thosai* until batter is used up.

8. Serve immediately with coconut chutney.

We call this Indian savoury doughnut. Nothing beats the taste of freshly fried *vada*, with its thin, crisp crust and creamy, fluffy interior. Tear it apart with your fingers and use it to scoop up a huge dollop of coconut chutney, and savour. Pure bliss.

VADA WITH COCONUT CHUTNEY

Makes 18–24 pieces

VADA

200 g (7 oz) urad dhal (black lentils), rinsed

1¹/₂ tsp salt, or to taste

1 tsp black mustard seeds, toasted

¹/₂ tsp cumin, toasted

2 green chillies, seeded and finely diced

¹/₂ medium onion, peeled and diced

1¹/₂ tsp sugar

Cooking oil as needed

COCONUT CHUTNEY

200 g (7 oz) grated skinned coconut

2 green chillies

1 medium onion, peeled and sliced

2 Tbsp cooking oil

1 tsp mustard seeds

4 dried chillies

2 stalks curry leaves, leaves plucked, stalks discarded

1 tsp salt

1 tsp sugar

125 ml (4 fl oz / ¹/₂ cup) water

1. Prepare coconut chutney. Using a food processor, lightly blend grated coconut, green chillies and onion. Transfer to a bowl.

2. Heat oil in a pan over medium heat. Add mustard seeds and when seeds begin to pop, add dried chillies and curry leaves. Fry for a minute, then add blended coconut mixture. Season with salt and sugar. Add 125 ml (4 fl oz / ¹/₂ cup) water and simmer over low heat for 5 minutes. Set aside to serve with *vada*.

3. Wash urad dhal several times and leave to soak in a large basin of water for at least 4 hours. Drain and place in a food processor. Add salt and blend to get a thick, smooth and fluffy paste. Scrape down sides of bowl a few times to ensure even consistency of paste.

4. Transfer paste to a large bowl and beat with a whisk in a clockwise direction for 30 seconds. This will aerate the paste for a fluffy *vada*. Test by dropping a small ball of paste in a bowl full of water. The ball should float if it is sufficiently aerated.

5. Add toasted mustard seeds, toasted cumin, green chillies, onion and sugar to paste. Mix well.

6. Heat some oil in a wok until it reaches 170°C. To test temperature, drop a tiny ball of paste into oil. If the paste rises to the surface in a few seconds, the oil is hot enough.

7. Using well-oiled hands, take a tablespoonful of paste and shape it into a ball. Slightly flatten the middle, then make a whole in the centre of *vada* with your thumb. Gently shake *vada* off your fingers into the hot oil. Deep-fry until *vada* is golden. Remove and drain well. Repeat until paste is used up.

8. Serve with coconut chutney.

FAVOURITE EURASIAN DISHES

This dish is also known as devil curry as it is fiery red and blistering hot. The addition of roast pork gives it a smoky edge. The cucumber helps to cool the taste buds and offers a reprieve from the spiciness of the curry. Despite its heat, you'll be wanting more after each bite!

CURRY DEBAL

Serves 6–8

1 kg (2 lb 3 oz) chicken, cut into chunks

¼ tsp dark soy sauce

1½ tsp salt

1 tsp ground white pepper

Cooking oil, as needed

200 g (7 oz) luncheon meat, cut into thick batons

1 large onion, peeled and thinly sliced

40 g (1⅓ oz) ginger, peeled and cut into thin strips

200 g (7 oz) roast pork, cut into thick batons

1 Tbsp mustard seeds, roughly pounded

1 tsp sugar

4 potatoes, peeled and cut into quarters

Water, as needed

250 g (9 oz) cabbage, cut into big chunks, leaves separated

1 cucumber, cut into thick batons

5 Tbsp white vinegar

SPICE PASTE

300 g (11 oz) shallots, peeled

4 cloves garlic, peeled

50 g (1¾ oz) ginger, peeled and sliced

10 red chillies

5 bird's eye chillies (*cili padi*), or to taste

50 g (1¾ oz) dried chillies

6 candlenuts

20 g (⅔ oz) turmeric, peeled

1. Season chicken with dark soy sauce, salt and pepper. Set aside to marinate for 30 minutes.

2. Using a food processor, blend all ingredients for spice paste until fine. Set aside.

3. Heat some oil in a pan over medium heat and fry luncheon meat until golden brown. Drain and set aside.

4. Leave 4 Tbsp oil in the pan and reheat over medium heat. Add onion and ginger and fry until fragrant.

5. Add roast pork and fry until lightly brown.

6. Add spice paste, mustard seeds and sugar and fry until oil separates from paste.

7. Add marinated chicken and continue frying until chicken changes colour.

8. Add potatoes and fried luncheon meat, then add enough water to cover chicken. Lower heat and simmer until chicken is cooked, potatoes are tender and curry is thickened.

9. Add cabbage and cucumber and continue to simmer for 10 minutes. Turn off heat.

10. Add vinegar and mix well.

11. Dish out, garnish as desired and serve.

Vindaloo is probably influenced by Portuguese cuisine where meat is often marinated in garlic and vinegar. This recipe is from my aunt who is of Eurasian-Portuguese descent, and the recipe-keeper of the family.

VINDALOO PORK RIBS

Serves 4–6

1 kg (2 lb 3 oz) pork ribs
4 Tbsp cooking oil
Water, as needed
2 tsp salt, or to taste
3 Tbsp white vinegar,
    or to taste

SPICE PASTE
200 g (7 oz) shallots, peeled
1 bulb garlic, peeled
40 g (1¹⁄₃ oz) ginger, peeled
15 dried chillies
3 Tbsp fennel
3 Tbsp cumin
1 Tbsp mustard seeds
1 Tbsp black peppercorns

1. Start preparations a day ahead.

2. Cut pork ribs into 5-cm (2-in) lengths and rinse.

3. Prepare spice paste. Using a food processor, blend all ingredients for spice paste until fine.

4. Marinate pork ribs with 2 Tbsp spice paste and set aside for 30 minutes.

5. Heat oil in a pot over medium heat. Add remaining spice paste and stir-fry until oil starts to separate from the paste and paste is fragrant.

6. Add pork ribs and stir-fry for 5 minutes.

7. Add enough water to cover pork ribs, then season with salt. Bring to a boil, then lower heat and simmer, covered, for 45 minutes or until pork ribs are tender. Stir occasionally to prevent burning.

8. When ribs are ready, stir in vinegar.

9. Set aside to cool, then refrigerate overnight and reheat before serving.

A hearty, sour savoury soup with tender gelatinous meat falling off the bones and a hint of brandy. In the olden days, this dish is usually served during celebratory occasions, given the cost of brandy.

PORK TROTTER AND SALTED VEGETABLE SOUP

Serves 4–6

150 g (5¹⁄₃ oz) salted pickled mustard (*kiam chye*)

1 pork trotter, about 450 g (1 lb), cleaned and cut into chunky pieces

1.5 litres (48 fl oz / 6 cups) water

2 sour plums

2 dried *assam* slices (*assam gelugur*)

1 bulb garlic

20 g (²⁄₃ oz) ginger, peeled and sliced

1 Tbsp sugar

2 Tbsp brandy

200 g (7 oz) soy sprouts, heads only

Salt, to taste

1. Soak salted pickled mustard for 3 hours to remove some of its saltiness. Change the water twice.

2. Blanch trotter in a pot of boiling water for 5 minutes to remove any scum, then rinse with cold water.

3. Place trotter in a pot with 1.5 litres (48 fl oz / 6 cups) water and add salted pickled mustard, sour plums, dried *assam* slices, garlic bulb and ginger. Bring to a boil.

4. Add sugar and 1 Tbsp brandy, then lower heat and simmer for 1¹⁄₂ hours or until trotter is tender.

5. Add heads of soy sprouts and simmer for another 5 minutes. Season with salt to taste.

6. Turn off heat and stir in remaining 1 Tbsp brandy.

7. Serve.

A perfect marriage of salty corned beef and sweet minced pork wrapped up in succulent tender cabbage and served in a flavourful chicken stock. It's good enough to serve on its own with steamed white rice, but can also be served as part of a meal with other dishes.

STEWED CABBAGE ROLLS

Serves 4–6

1 medium head cabbage

2 Tbsp cooking oil

1 medium yellow onion, peeled and cut into quarters

1 cinnamon stick

6 black peppercorns

1 star anise

4 cloves

1 litre (32 fl oz / 4 cups) chicken stock

FILLING

600 g (1 lb 5⅓ oz) minced pork belly

200 g (7 oz) corned beef

1 egg

25 g (⅘ oz) cream crackers, crushed

2 spring onions, thinly sliced

2 Tbsp Chinese rice wine (*hua tiao jiu*)

½ tsp salt

1 tsp ground white pepper

½ tsp sugar

1. Boil water in a pot large enough to submerge whole cabbage. Using a small knife, core cabbage and place into boiling water. The leaves will gradually separate. Lower heat to simmer until cabbage leaves have softened. Remove leaves and place on a tray to cool.

2. Cut off the thick centre rib from each leaf to make it easier to roll up if necessary.

3. Prepare filling. Mix minced pork belly well with corned beef, egg, cream cracker crumbs, spring onions, Chinese rice wine, salt, pepper and sugar.

4. Place 1 Tbsp filling on a cabbage leaf and roll leaf up to enclose mixture. Secure roll with butcher's twine. Repeat until ingredients are used up.

5. Heat oil in saucepan over medium heat. Add onion, cinnamon, peppercorns, star anise and cloves. Stir-fry until fragrant and onion is soft.

6. Add chicken stock and bring to a boil. Lower heat to a simmer.

7. Gently lower cabbage rolls into stock and simmer for 8–10 minutes until filling is cooked.

8. Top stock up with more water if needed. Taste and adjust seasoning with more salt.

9. Serve cabbage rolls in stock and garnish as desired.

The stewed pineapple imparts a piquant sweetness to the rich spiced coconut curry
that pairs extremely well with the fresh succulent prawns.
Enjoy with a bowl of piping hot steamed rice.

PRAWN AND PINEAPPLE CURRY

Serves 4–6

Cooking oil, as needed

1/2 tsp sugar

400 ml (13 1/2 fl oz) water

1/2 medium pineapple, peeled
and cut into wedges

3 dried *assam* slices
(*assam gelugur*)

300 ml (10 fl oz / 1 1/4 cups)
coconut milk

1 kg (2 lb 3 oz) large prawns,
cleaned, legs and feelers
trimmed

1 tsp salt

SPICE PASTE

8 dried chillies

3 red bird's eye chillies
(*cili padi*)

150 g (5 1/3 oz) shallots,
peeled

2 cloves garlic

3 candlenuts

10 g (1/3 oz) ginger, peeled

15 g (1/2 oz) galangal, peeled

40 g (1 1/3 oz) turmeric, peeled

2 stalks lemongrass, ends
trimmed

1 tsp *belacan* (dried prawn
paste), toasted

40 g (1 1/3 oz) dried prawns,
soaked to soften

1. Using a food processor, blend all ingredients
    for spice paste until fine.

2. Heat 4 Tbsp oil in a pan over medium heat.
    Add spice paste and sugar and stir-fry until oil
    separates from paste.

3. Add 400 ml (13 1/3 fl oz) water, pineapple and
    dried *assam* slices. Lower heat and simmer for
    10 minutes.

4. Add two-thirds of coconut milk and simmer for
    another 4 minutes. Stir frequently so mixture
    does not boil. This will prevent the coconut milk
    from curdling.

5. Add prawns and season with salt. Continue to
    simmer for another 5 minutes until prawns are
    cooked.

6. Add remaining coconut milk and stir to mix.
    Adjust seasoning to taste.

7. Dish out and serve.

Sugee cake is a must-have for every festive occasion in Eurasian homes.
Our version is light and moist with a lovely bite from the semolina and ground almonds.
A simple butter icing adds a buttery sweetness to the cake.

SUGEE CAKE

Makes one 20-cm (8-in) square cake

250 g (9 oz) butter

180 g (6½ oz) castor sugar

50 g (1¾ oz) plain flour

120 g (4⅓ oz) semolina

120 g (4⅓ oz) ground almonds

½ tsp vanilla paste or essence

6 egg yolks

2 egg whites

BUTTER ICING

150 g (5⅓ oz) butter

300 g (11 oz) icing sugar

2 Tbsp milk

1. In a mixing bowl, cream butter and castor sugar until light and fluffy.

2. Fold in plain flour, semolina, ground almonds and vanilla paste or essence. Cover and let rest for at least 2 hours, but not more than 6 hours.

3. Preheat oven to 180°C (350°F). Grease and line a 20-cm (8-in) square baking pan.

4. Add egg yolks to rested mixture and mix well. Set batter aside.

5. In a clean bowl, whisk egg whites until soft peaks form. Fold beaten egg whites into batter.

6. Pour batter into prepared baking pan and bake for 30 minutes or until a skewer inserted into the centre of cake comes out clean.

7. Leave cake to rest in pan for 10 minutes before removing to cool completely on a wire rack.

8. Prepare butter icing. Beat butter in a large bowl until softened. Add half the icing sugar and beat until smooth. Add remaining icing sugar and milk and beat until mixture is smooth and creamy.

9. Spread butter icing over top of cooled cake. Slice and serve.

FAVOURITE PERANAKAN DISHES

A rich and fragrant stew made with chicken, potatoes, caramelised shallots and fermented soy bean paste. Perfect with a bowl of piping hot steamed white rice. The flavours of this stew develop with keeping, so don't fret if there are leftovers. Reheat to enjoy the following day.

AYAM PONGTEH

Serves 4–6

1 whole chicken, 1–1.2 kg (2 lb 3 oz–2 lb 6 oz)

12 dried Chinese mushrooms

250 g (9 oz) shallots, peeled

60 g (2 oz) garlic, peeled

4 Tbsp cooking oil

5 Tbsp fermented soy bean paste (*tau cheo*)

20 g (²/₃ oz) coriander powder

4 potatoes, peeled and cut into quarters

¹/₂ tsp sugar

1 tsp dark soy sauce

2 Tbsp light soy sauce

1. Rinse chicken and cut into chunks. Set aside.

2. Rinse and soak dried Chinese mushrooms in at least 250 ml (8 fl oz / 1 cup) water until softened. Trim stems and discard. Reserve 250 ml (8 fl oz / 1 cup) soaking liquid for use in stew.

3. Using a food processor, grind shallots and garlic into a paste.

4. Heat oil in a pan over medium heat. Add shallot and garlic paste and stir-fry until fragrant and oil starts to separate from the paste.

5. Add fermented soy bean paste and coriander powder. Fry for another minute until fragrant.

6. Add chicken and mix until meat changes colour.

7. Add potatoes and mix to coat potatoes with paste.

8. Season with sugar, dark soy sauce and light soy sauce. Fry for another minute.

9. Add reserved mushroom soaking liquid and top up with more water to just cover chicken.

10. Bring mixture to a boil, then lower heat, cover pan and let simmer for 20–25 minutes until chicken is cooked through and potatoes are tender.

11. Dish out, garnish as desired and serve.

Buah keluak used to be known as opium fruit as the untreated nuts are poisonous. The nuts that are commercially available today have already been processed. All it needs is some scrubbing and soaking to remove residual ash and grit from the cleaning process. These nuts have a bitter taste similar to that of dark, unsweetened chocolate. Cooked in a thick tamarind gravy, it is just divine.

BABI BUAH KELUAK

Serves 6

30 *buah keluak* (Indonesian black nuts)

Salt, as needed

Sugar, as needed

50 g (1³⁄₄ oz) minced pork

50 g (1³⁄₄ oz) minced prawn

30 g (1 oz) carrot, peeled and finely diced

1 water chestnut, peeled and finely diced

A pinch of cornflour

Egg white from 1 egg

1 kg (2 lb 3 oz) pork ribs

3 Tbsp tamarind paste

1 litre (32 fl oz / 4 cups) water

4 Tbsp cooking oil

2 stalks lemongrass, ends trimmed and bruised

4 kaffir lime leaves

SPICE PASTE

25 dried chillies, soaked to soften

250 g (9 oz) shallots, peeled

6 cloves garlic, peeled

20 g (²⁄₃ oz) ginger, peeled

20 g (²⁄₃ oz) turmeric, peeled

45 g (1¹⁄₂ oz) galangal, peeled

5 stalks lemongrass, ends trimmed and bruised

1 tsp *belacan* (dried shrimp paste), toasted

8 candlenuts

1. Prepare *buah keluak* ahead. Scrub and rinse nuts, then set aside to soak for 5 days. Change water daily.

2. Using a pestle, crack top end of nuts and make a small opening. Using a small spoon, scoop out flesh into a bowl. Check that there are no bits of cracked shell in the flesh. Reserve shells.

3. Add ¹⁄₄ tsp salt and a pinch of sugar to *buah keluak* flesh and pound using a mortar and pestle. Transfer to a bowl, then add minced pork, minced prawn, carrot, water chestnut, cornflour and egg white. Mix well. Stuff mixture into shells and refrigerate.

4. Add all ingredients for spice paste into a food processor and blend until fine.

5. Place pork ribs in a bowl and mix well with 1 Tbsp spice paste. Set aside to marinate for 30 minutes.

6. Mix tamarind paste with 1 litre (32 fl oz / 4 cups) water and strain. Discard any fibre and seeds. Set aside.

7. Heat oil in a pan over medium heat. Add spice paste, 1 tsp sugar and lemongrass and stir-fry until oil starts to separate from paste and paste is fragrant.

8. Add marinated pork ribs and stir-fry until ribs change colour.

9. Add tamarind water, 2 tsp salt and kaffir lime leaves. Lower heat and simmer until liquid is reduced by half.

10. Add *buah keluak*, then cover pot with a lid and simmer for 30 minutes until pork ribs are tender.

11. Season to taste with salt and sugar. Dish out, garnish as desired and serve.

TIP   When selecting *buah keluak*, choose those that are heavy. The flesh inside the shell should not move around when the nut is shaken. Buy more than required in the recipe as some nuts may turn out to be bad. If using store-bought *buah keluak* flesh and empty shells, you will need 250 g (9 oz) flesh for this recipe. Boil and scrub the empty shells well before using.

What sets Nyonya *chap chye* apart from other Chinese vegetable stews is the addition of fermented soy bean paste. This is also what gives this stew its alluring flavour. Like *ayam pongteh* (page xx), this can be enjoyed simply with bowl of piping hot steamed white rice.

NYONYA CHAP CHYE VEGETABLE STEW

Serves 6–8

10 dried Chinese mushrooms

20 g (²/₃ oz) dried wood ear fungus

40 g (1¹/₃ oz) dried bean curd sticks

30 g (1 oz) glass noodles

20 g (²/₃ oz) dried lily buds

500 g (1 lb 1¹/₂ oz) cabbage

1 carrot, peeled

100 g (3¹/₂ oz) baby corn

2 Tbsp cooking oil

6 cloves garlic, peeled and minced

2 Tbsp fermented soy bean paste (*tau cheo*)

250 ml (8 fl oz / 1 cup) water

¹/₂ tsp sugar

¹/₂ tsp salt, or to taste

1. Soak dried Chinese mushrooms, wood ear fungus, dried bean curd sticks, glass noodles and dried lily buds separately in water for about 10 minutes, or until softened. Drain and set aside.

2. Trim and discard mushrooms stalks, then cut mushroom caps into halves or thirds. Trim and discard any hard bits from wood ear fungus, then cut into bite-size pieces. Cut bean curd sticks into 5-cm (2-in) lengths. Cut glass noodles into 10-cm (4-in) lengths. Trim and discard hard ends of dried lily buds and tie each one into a knot.

3. Slice cabbage into 3-cm (1¹/₅-in) pieces. Cut carrot into rounds and trim into floral shapes if desired.

4. Heat oil in a wok over medium heat. Add garlic and stir-fry until fragrant. Add fermented soy bean paste and stir-fry to mix.

5. Add dried Chinese mushrooms and wood ear fungus. Stir-fry for a minute.

6. Add cabbage, carrot and baby corn. Stir-fry for a minute.

7. Add dried bean curd sticks, glass noodles and dried lily buds and stir-fry for another minute.

8. Add 250 ml (8 fl oz / 1 cup) water, sugar and salt. Stir-fry to mix.

9. Cover wok with a lid and lower heat to simmer until cabbage is softened.

10. Dish out and serve.

We love how the fish maw soaks up the broth, allowing you to enjoy all the flavours of the soup in one mouthful. This luxurious dish is often served during Chinese New Year, but there's no reason why we can't enjoy this at other times of the year too!

FISH MAW SOUP

Serves 6–8

60 g (2 oz) fish maw, soaked in hot water to soften

5 g (1/6 oz) dried wood ear fungus, soaked to soften

200 g (7 oz) yam bean, peeled and sliced

50 g (1¾ oz) carrot, peeled and sliced

1 small bamboo shoot, peeled and sliced

100 g (3½ oz) cabbage, cut into 5-cm (2-in) strips

3 Tbsp cooking oil

6 cloves garlic, peeled and minced

STOCK

3 chicken carcasses

3 litres (96 fl oz / 12 cups) water

2 slices ginger

1 spring onion

3 small dried scallops

PRAWN PASTE

450 g (1 lb) peeled prawns

1½ Tbsp tapioca flour

½ tsp salt

¼ tsp ground white pepper

⅛ tsp sugar

FISH PASTE OMELETTE ROLLS

3 eggs

Salt, as needed

Ground white pepper, as needed

150 g (5⅓ oz) fresh fish paste

1. Prepare stock. Blanch chicken carcasses in boiling water for 5 minutes, then rinse with running water. Place chicken carcasses in a large pot and add 3 litres (96 fl oz / 12 cups) water, ginger, spring onion and dried scallops. Bring to a boil, then lower heat and simmer for 1 hour or until stock is reduced by half. Strain stock back into pot. Set aside.

2. Place ingredients for prawn paste in a food processor and blend into a paste. Transfer to a bowl. Using a spatula, beat prawn paste in a clockwise direction until you feel some resistance and the paste is sticky. Cover bowl and let rest in the refrigerator until needed.

3. Prepare fish paste omelette rolls. Whisk eggs in a bowl and season with a pinch of salt and pepper. Heat a non-stick pan over low heat. Spoon a ladle of egg mixture into pan, then swirl to create a thin sheet. Cook until underside is browned. Remove and set egg sheet aside on a plate to cool. Repeat until eggs are used up.

4. Spread a thin layer of fish paste on each egg sheet, then roll each one up tightly. Steam rolls for 15 minutes, then set aside to cool. Cut cooled rolls diagonally into bite-size pieces. Set aside.

5. Squeeze excess water from soaked fish maw and cut into pieces. Trim and discard hard bits from soaked dried wood ear fungus, then cut into pieces.

6. Return stock to a boil.

7. Dip 2 metal teaspoons into water, then use to spoon and shape rested prawn paste into balls. Drop balls into boiling stock.

8. Add fish maw, yam bean, carrot, dried wood ear fungus and bamboo shoot. Simmer for a minute. Add cabbage and continue to simmer until softened.

9. Heat oil in a pan over medium heat. Add garlic and stir-fry until fragrant. Serve soup hot, garnished with garlic and garlic oil.

This vegetable pickle can be made ahead and kept refrigerated in an airtight jar.
It is perfect served as a side dish with meals or as an appetiser. Its lovely crunchy texture
also makes it great as a snack whenever you feel the need to munch on something!

ACAR VEGETABLE PICKLE

Serves 6–8

4 Tbsp cooking oil

150 ml (5 fl oz) white vinegar

8 Tbsp sugar

1 Tbsp salt

100 g (3¹/₃ oz) peanuts, toasted
  and crushed

40 g (1¹/₃ oz) white sesame
  seeds, toasted

VEGETABLES

1 medium cucumber

2 medium carrots

500 g (1 lb 1¹/₂ oz) white
  cabbage

150 g (5¹/₃ oz) long beans

200 g (7 oz) cauliflower

200 g (7 oz) pineapple

4 red chillies

4 green chillies

1 tsp salt

BLANCHING LIQUID

1 litre (32 fl oz / 4 cups) water

500 ml (16 fl oz / 2 cups)
  white vinegar

1 Tbsp salt

2 Tbsp sugar

SPICE PASTE

25 dried chillies, soaked
  to soften

150 g (5¹/₃ oz) shallots, peeled

20 g (²/₃ oz) garlic, peeled

15 g (¹/₂ oz) turmeric, peeled

10 g (¹/₃ oz) galangal, peeled

4 candlenuts

20 g (²/₃ oz) *belacan* (dried
  prawn paste), toasted

2 stalks lemongrass

1. Prepare vegetables. Cut cucumber in half, then
   remove and discard core. Cut cucumber into 5-cm
   (2-in) strips. Peel carrots and cut into 5-cm (2-in)
   strips. Cut cabbage into 4-cm (1¹/₂-in) pieces. Cut
   long beans into 5-cm (2-in) lengths. Cut cauliflower
   into small florets. Cut pineapple into small pieces.
   Half chillies lengthwise and remove seeds.

2. Rub salt into carrot and cucumber strips. Set aside
   to rest for 1 hour, then wrap carrot and cucumber
   strips in a clean kitchen towel or muslin cloth and
   squeeze dry. Set aside.

3. Combine all ingredients for blanching liquid in a
   pot and bring to a rapid boil. Blanch cabbage, long
   beans, cauliflower and chillies separately for
   10 seconds, then drain and pat dry. Arrange
   blanched vegetables in a single layer on a tray
   and sun for 2 hours.

4. Combine all ingredients for spice paste in a food
   processor and blend until fine.

5. Heat oil in a wok over medium heat. Add spice paste
   and stir-fry for 5–6 minutes until mixture is fragrant.
   Remove and set aside to cool.

6. In a bowl, mix vinegar with sugar and salt. Add
   cooled spice paste and mix well. Adjust seasoning
   to taste.

7. Combine vegetables in a large bowl. Add vinegar
   mixture and mix until vegetables are well-coated.
   Add peanuts and sesame seeds. Mix well.

8. Serve immediately or refrigerate overnight for the
   flavours to develop.

Bubur cha cha can be enjoyed hot or cold. This is one of our favourite sweet desserts, made more luxurious by adding succulent, rich creamy durian. Using the different types of sweet potato and yam add a dash of colour, while tapioca cubes and sago pearls add texture.

BUBUR CHA CHA WITH DURIAN

Serves 8–10

50 g (1³/₄ oz) black-eyed beans

200 g (7 oz) yam

150 g (5¹/₃ oz) purple sweet potato

150 g (5¹/₃ oz) orange sweet potato

150 g (5¹/₃ oz) yellow sweet potato

100 g (3¹/₂ oz) tapioca flour cubes

40 g (1¹/₃ oz) sago pearls

1 litre (32 fl oz / 4 cups) water

200 g (7 oz) rock sugar

800 ml (26²/₃ fl oz) coconut milk

4–5 pandan leaves, knotted

A pinch of salt, or to taste

1 large durian

1. Soak black-eyed beans in hot water for 2 hours, then boil for 15–20 minutes. Drain and set aside.

2. Peel yam and sweet potatoes, and cut into cubes. Place in a steamer and steam over high heat until tender. Set aside.

3. Boil a pot of water and add tapioca flour cubes. Lower heat and simmer until cubes are cooked and float. Remove and place in a bowl of cool water.

4. Return water to the boil and cook sago pearls for about 10 minutes, stirring periodically. The sago pearls will not be fully done at this point. Drain and set aside.

5. Bring 1 litre (32 fl oz / 4 cups) water to a simmer in a pot. Add sago pearls, rock sugar and pandan leaves. Stir until rock sugar is dissolved and sago pearls are mostly translucent. Keep mixture simmering over low heat and stir in coconut milk. Do not allow mixture to boil as this will cause coconut milk to split.

6. Add black-eyed beans, tapioca flour cubes, yam cubes and sweet potato cubes. Season with salt.

7. Serve hot or refrigerate and serve chilled. Ladle into bowls and top with a luscious creamy seed of durian.

WEIGHTS AND MEASURES

Quantities for this book are given in metric, imperial and American (spoon and cup) measures. Standard spoon and cup measurements used are: 1 teaspoon = 5 ml, 1 tablespoon = 15 ml and 1 cup = 250 ml. All measures are level unless otherwise stated.

LIQUID AND VOLUME MEASURES

Metric	Imperial	American
5 ml	$1/6$ fl oz	1 teaspoon
10 ml	$1/3$ fl oz	1 dessertspoon
15 ml	$1/2$ fl oz	1 tablespoon
60 ml	2 fl oz	$1/4$ cup (4 tablespoons)
85 ml	$2^1/2$ fl oz	$1/3$ cup
90 ml	3 fl oz	$3/8$ cup (6 tablespoons)
125 ml	4 fl oz	$1/2$ cup
180 ml	6 fl oz	$3/4$ cup
250 ml	8 fl oz	1 cup
300 ml	10 fl oz ($1/2$ pint)	$1^1/4$ cups
375 ml	12 fl oz	$1^1/2$ cups
435 ml	14 fl oz	$1^3/4$ cups
500 ml	16 fl oz	2 cups
625 ml	20 fl oz (1 pint)	$2^1/2$ cups
750 ml	24 fl oz ($1^1/5$ pints)	3 cups
1 litre	32 fl oz ($1^3/5$ pints)	4 cups
1.25 litres	40 fl oz (2 pints)	5 cups
1.5 litres	48 fl oz ($2^2/5$ pints)	6 cups
2.5 litres	80 fl oz (4 pints)	10 cups

DRY MEASURES

Metric	Imperial
30 grams	1 ounce
45 grams	$1^1/2$ ounces
55 grams	2 ounces
70 grams	$2^1/2$ ounces
85 grams	3 ounces
100 grams	$3^1/2$ ounces
110 grams	4 ounces
125 grams	$4^1/2$ ounces
140 grams	5 ounces
280 grams	10 ounces
450 grams	16 ounces (1 pound)
500 grams	1 pound, $1^1/2$ ounces
700 grams	$1^1/2$ pounds
800 grams	$1^3/4$ pounds
1 kilogram	2 pounds, 3 ounces
1.5 kilograms	3 pounds, $4^1/2$ ounces
2 kilograms	4 pounds, 6 ounces

LENGTH

Metric	Imperial
0.5 cm	$1/4$ inch
1 cm	$1/2$ inch
1.5 cm	$3/4$ inch
2.5 cm	1 inch

OVEN TEMPERATURE

	°C	°F	Gas Regulo
Very slow	120	250	1
Slow	150	300	2
Moderately slow	160	325	3
Moderate	180	350	4
Moderately hot	190/200	370/400	5/6
Hot	210/220	410/440	6/7
Very hot	230	450	8
Super hot	250/290	475/550	9/10

ABBREVIATION

tsp	teaspoon
Tbsp	tablespoon
g	gram
kg	kilogram
ml	millilitre